Piano Solo

Piano Solos
for All Occasions
The Complete Resource for Every Pianist!

D1452945

ISBN 0-634-05681-6

HAL•LEONARD® CORPORATION
7777 W. BLUEMOUND RD. P.O. BOX 13819 MILWAUKEE, WI 53213

Visit Hal Leonard Online at
www.halleonard.com

CONTENTS

EDELWEISS
from THE SOUND OF MUSIC

Lyrics by OSCAR HAMMERSTEIN II
Music by RICHARD RODGERS

Moderately and expressively

IT'S A GRAND NIGHT FOR SINGING

from STATE FAIR

Lyrics by OSCAR HAMMERSTEIN II
Music by RICHARD RODGERS

MEMORY
from CATS

Music by ANDREW LLOYD WEBBER
Text by TREVOR NUNN after T.S. ELIOT

PEOPLE WILL SAY WE'RE IN LOVE

from OKLAHOMA!

Lyrics by OSCAR HAMMERSTEIN II
Music by RICHARD RODGERS

Moderately, in a singing style

Broadly

Largamente

8va

loco

8va

SHALL WE DANCE?

from THE KING AND I

Lyrics by OSCAR HAMMERSTEIN II
Music by RICHARD RODGERS

Brightly

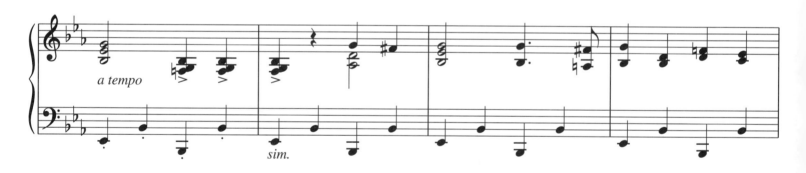

SOME ENCHANTED EVENING

from SOUTH PACIFIC

Lyrics by OSCAR HAMMERSTEIN II
Music by RICHARD RODGERS

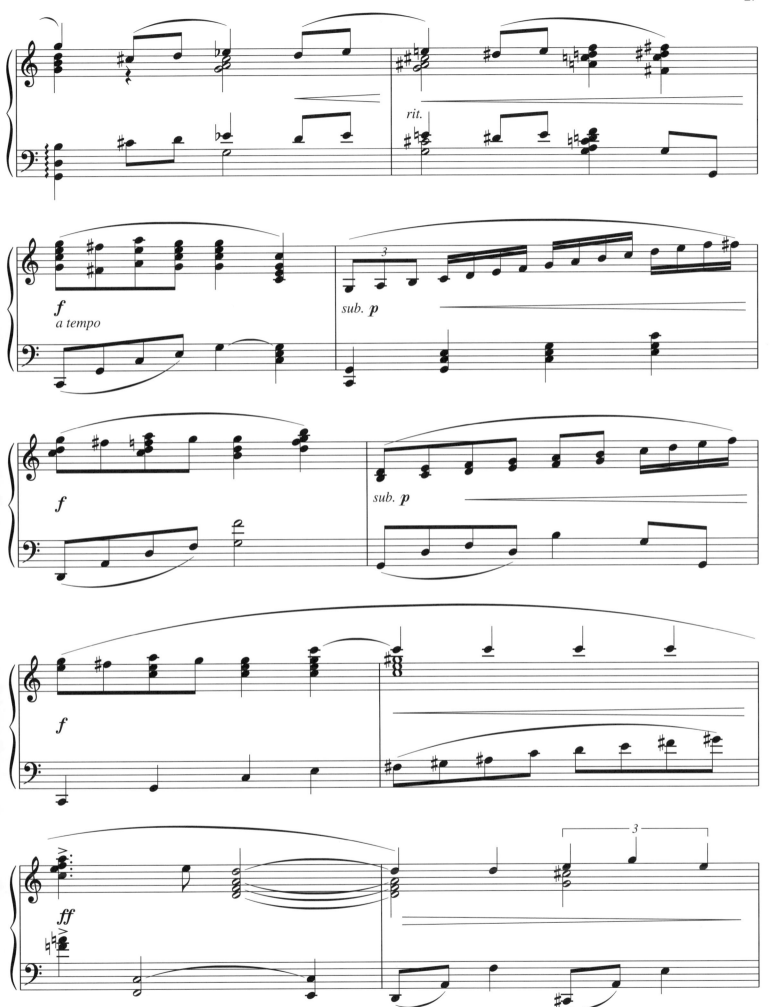

8vb

YOU'LL NEVER WALK ALONE
from CAROUSEL

Lyrics by OSCAR HAMMERSTEIN II
Music by RICHARD RODGERS

Moderately, with expression

FÜR ELISE

By LUDWIG VAN BEETHOVEN

34

IN THE HALL OF THE MOUNTAIN KING

from PEER GYNT

By EDVARD GRIEG

Alla marcia e molto marcato

38

JESU, JOY OF MAN'S DESIRING

By JOHANN SEBASTIAN BACH

42

RONDEAU

By JEAN-JOSEPH MOURET

SOLFEGGIETTO

By CARL PHILIPP EMANUEL BACH

Non troppo vivo

TALES FROM THE VIENNA WOODS

By JOHANN STRAUSS, JR.

52

SONATA IN A MAJOR, L. 483

By DOMENICO SCARLATTI

[Allegro]

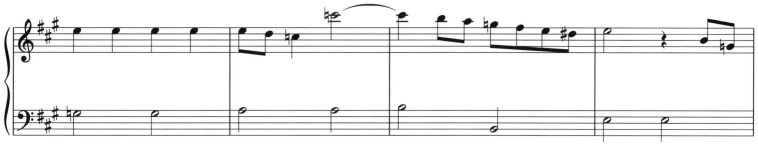

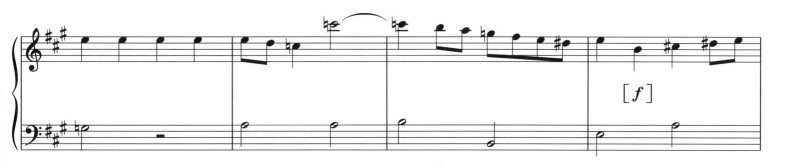

WALTZ IN C# MINOR

By FREDERIC CHOPIN

Tempo giusto

Più mosso

ALL BLUES

By MILES DAVIS

D.C. al Coda
(with repeat)

CODA

DON'T GET AROUND MUCH ANYMORE

Words and Music by DUKE ELLINGTON
and BOB RUSSELL

GEORGIA ON MY MIND

Words by STUART GORRELL
Music by HOAGY CARMICHAEL

HAVE YOU MET MISS JONES?

from I'D RATHER BE RIGHT

Words by LORENZ HART
Music by RICHARD RODGERS

IT DON'T MEAN A THING

(If It Ain't Got That Swing)

from SOPHISTICATED LADIES

Words and Music by DUKE ELLINGTON
and IRVING MILLS

84

no pedal

mf

grad. cresc.

f

mp   grad. cresc.

f

add pedal

ROUTE 66

By BOBBY TROUP

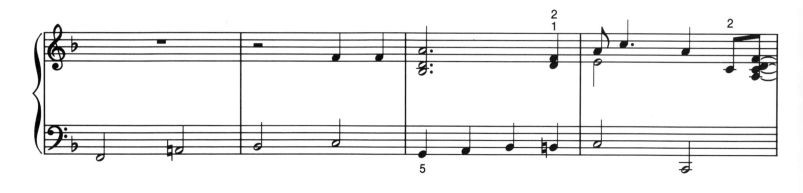

STELLA BY STARLIGHT
from the Paramount Picture THE UNINVITED

Words by NED WASHINGTON
Music by VICTOR YOUNG

Moderately slow, expressively

smoothly

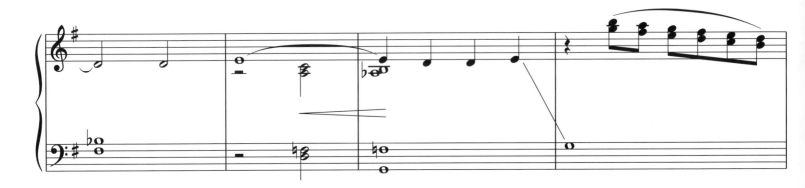

Steady, flowing tempo

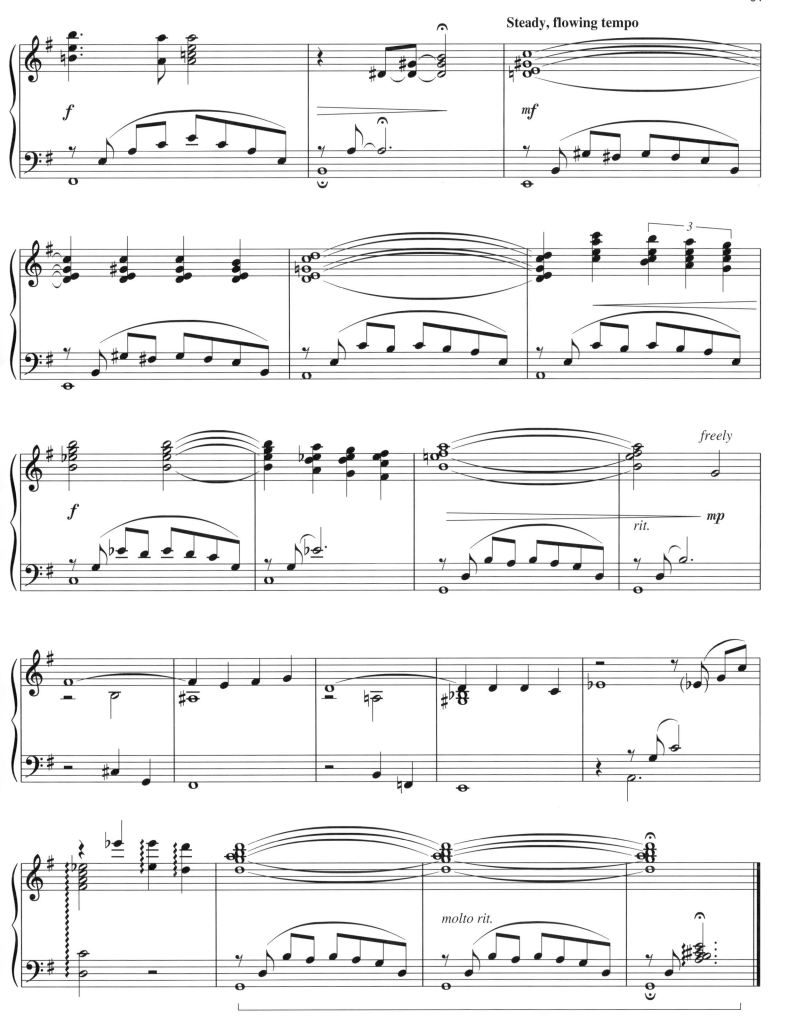

STORMY WEATHER

(Keeps Rainin' All the Time)
from COTTON CLUB PARADE OF 1933

Lyric by TED KOEHLER
Music by HAROLD ARLEN

94

A DAY IN THE LIFE OF A FOOL
(Manha de Carnaval)

Words by CARL SIGMAN
Music by LUIZ BONFA

Bossa Nova

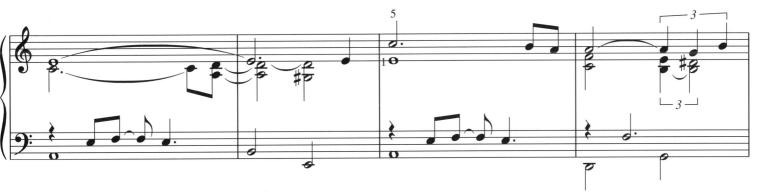

THE GIRL FROM IPANEMA
(Garôta de Ipanema)

Music by ANTONIO CARLOS JOBIM
English Words by NORMAN GIMBEL
Original Words by VINICIUS DE MORAES

Bossa Nova; playfully (♩ = 92)

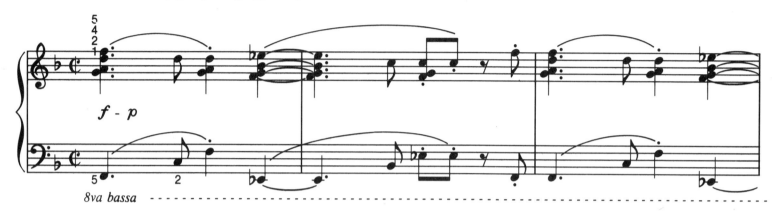

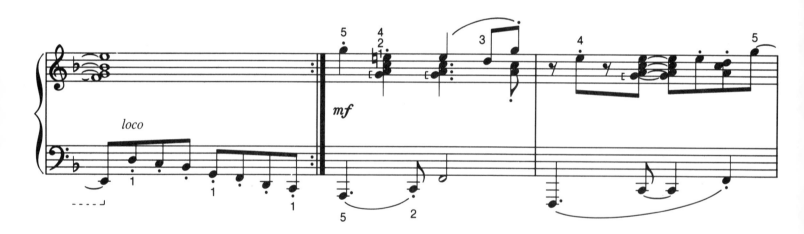

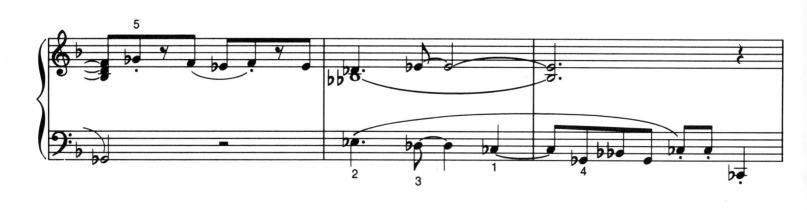

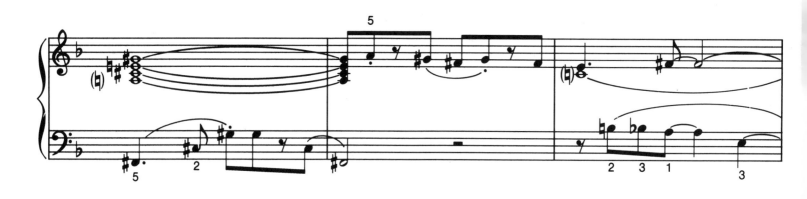

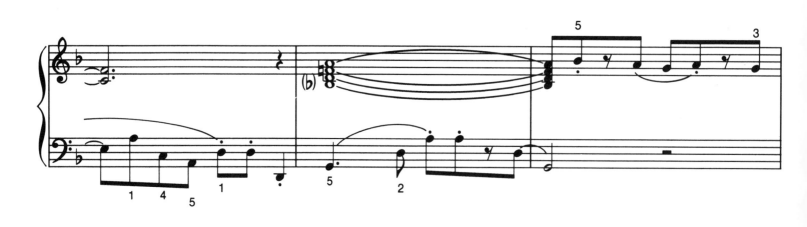

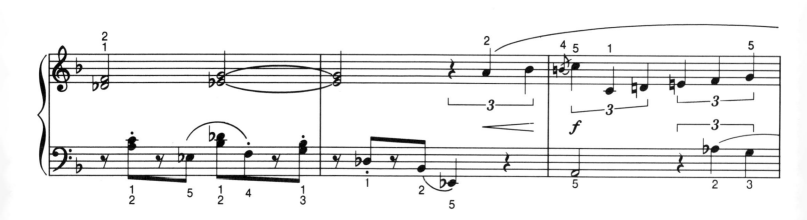

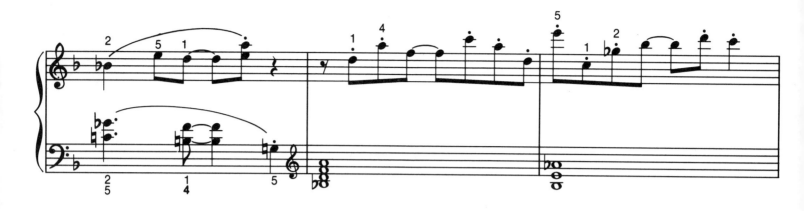

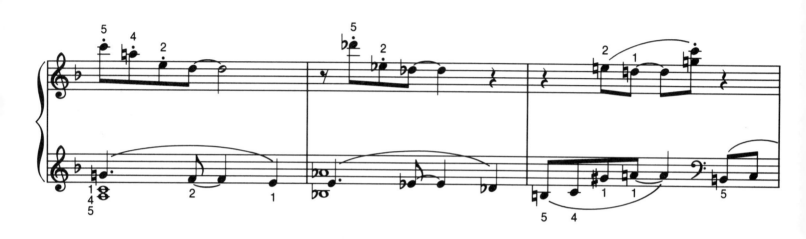

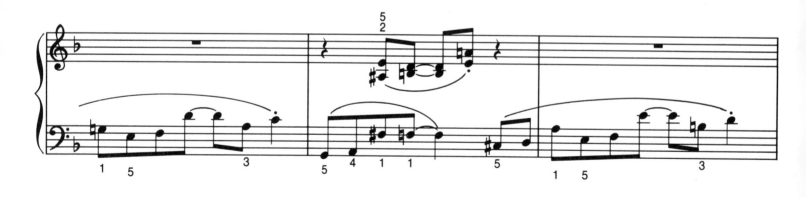

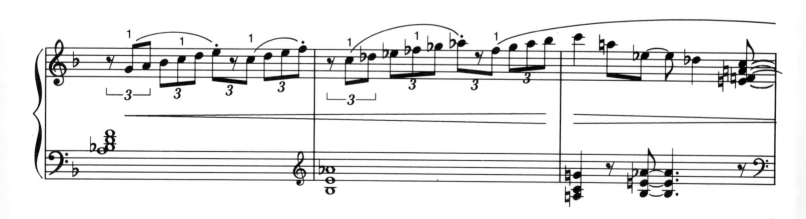

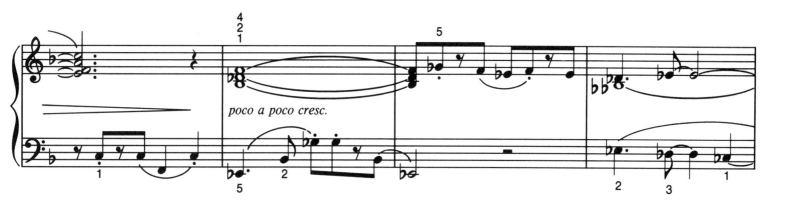

poco a poco cresc.

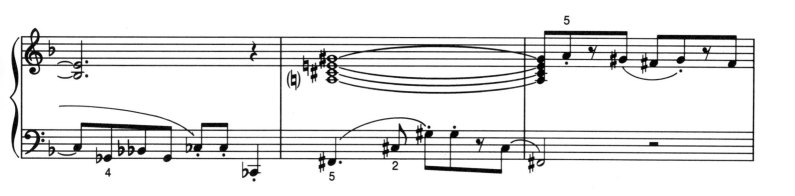

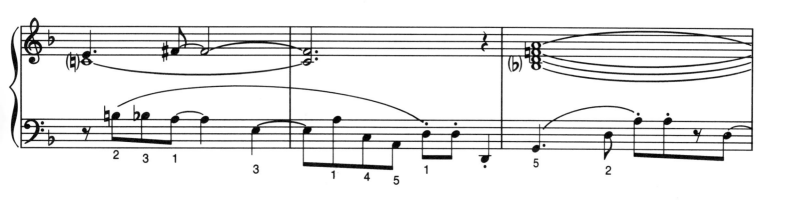

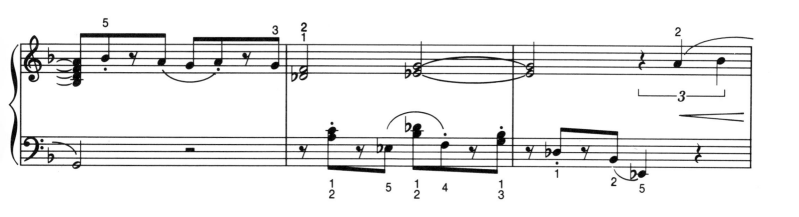

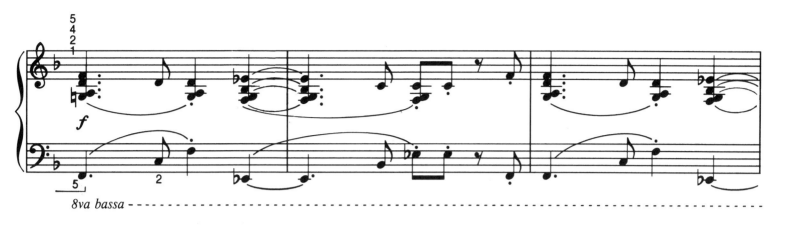

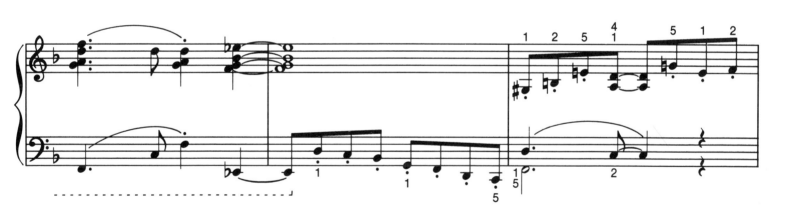

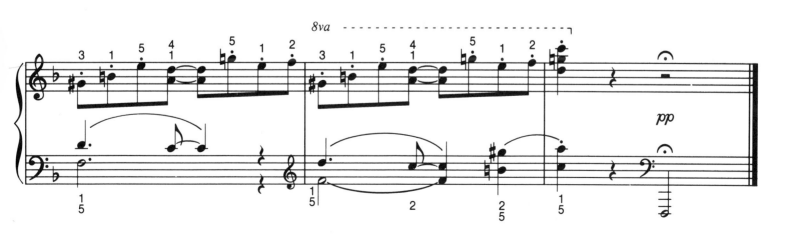

HOW INSENSITIVE
(Insensatez)

Music by ANTONIO CARLOS JOBIM
Original Words by VINICIUS DE MORAES
English Words by NORMAN GIMBEL

Moderately slow

with pedal

MEDITATION
(Meditacáo)

Music by ANTONIO CARLOS JOBIM
Original Words by NEWTON MENDONCA
English Words by NORMAN GIMBEL

Relaxed Bossa Nova

To Coda

D.S. al Coda

CODA

ONCE I LOVED
(Amor em Paz)
(Love in Peace)

Music by ANTONIO CARLOS JOBIM
Portuguese Lyrics by VINICIUS DE MORAES
English Lyrics by RAY GILBERT

120

D.S. al Coda

CODA

Freely

SO NICE
(Summer Samba)

Original Words and Music by MARCOS VALLE
and PAULO SERGIO VALLE
English Words by NORMAN GIMBEL

Medium Bossa Nova

WATCH WHAT HAPPENS
from THE UMBRELLAS OF CHERBOURG

Music by MICHEL LEGRAND
Original French Text by JACQUES DEMY
English Lyrics by NORMAN GIMBEL

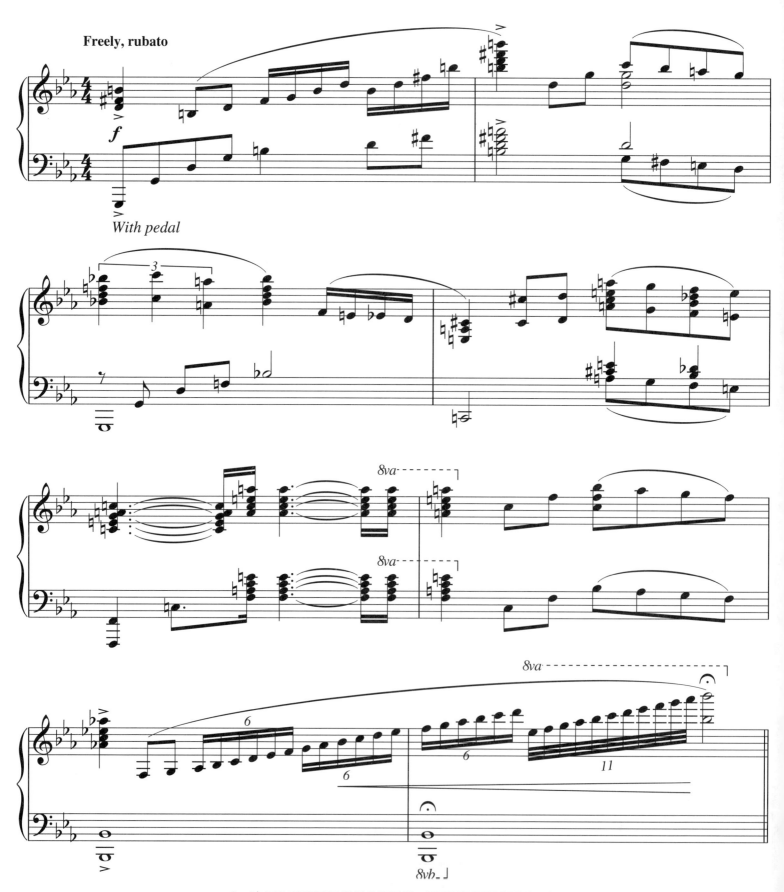

Easy Bossa Nova

THE ANNIVERSARY WALTZ

Words and Music by AL DUBIN
and DAVE FRANKLIN

Moderate Waltz

With pedal

ALL I ASK OF YOU
from THE PHANTOM OF THE OPERA

Music by ANDREW LLOYD WEBBER
Lyrics by CHARLES HART
Additional Lyrics by RICHARD STILGOE

Andante

molto rit.

f a tempo

Grandioso

broaden

ff

mp

molto rit.

8vb

AVE MARIA

By FRANZ SCHUBERT

Molto lento

BRIDAL CHORUS
from LOHENGRIN

By RICHARD WAGNER

Moderato

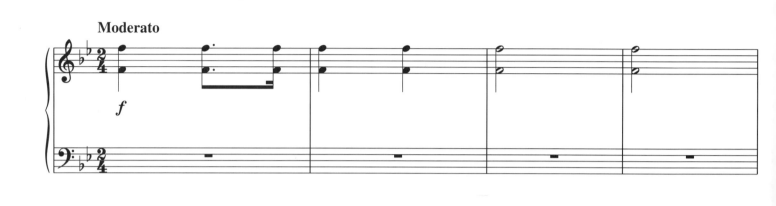

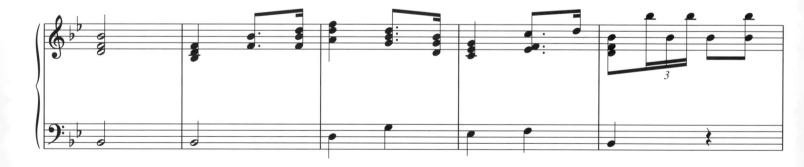

CANON IN D

By JOHANN PACHELBEL

THE LORD'S PRAYER

By ALBERT HAY MALOTTE

Reverently, somewhat rubato

Majestically, slightly brighter

ROMEO AND JULIET
(Love Theme)
from the Paramount Picture ROMEO AND JULIET

By NINO ROTA

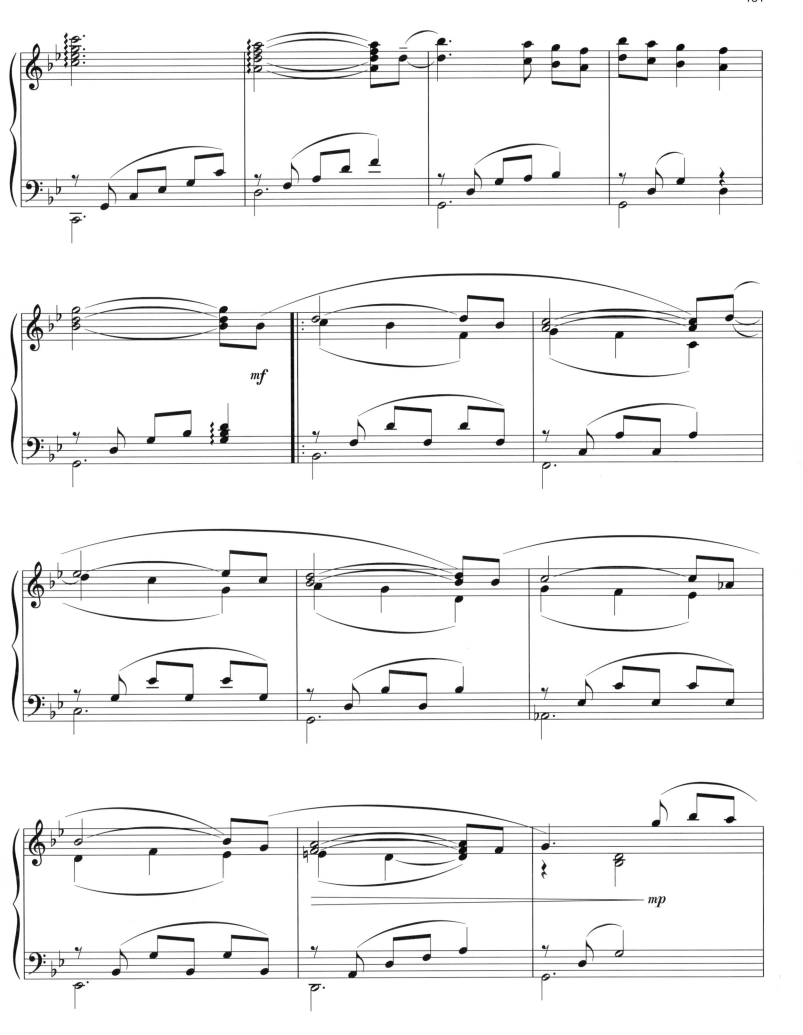

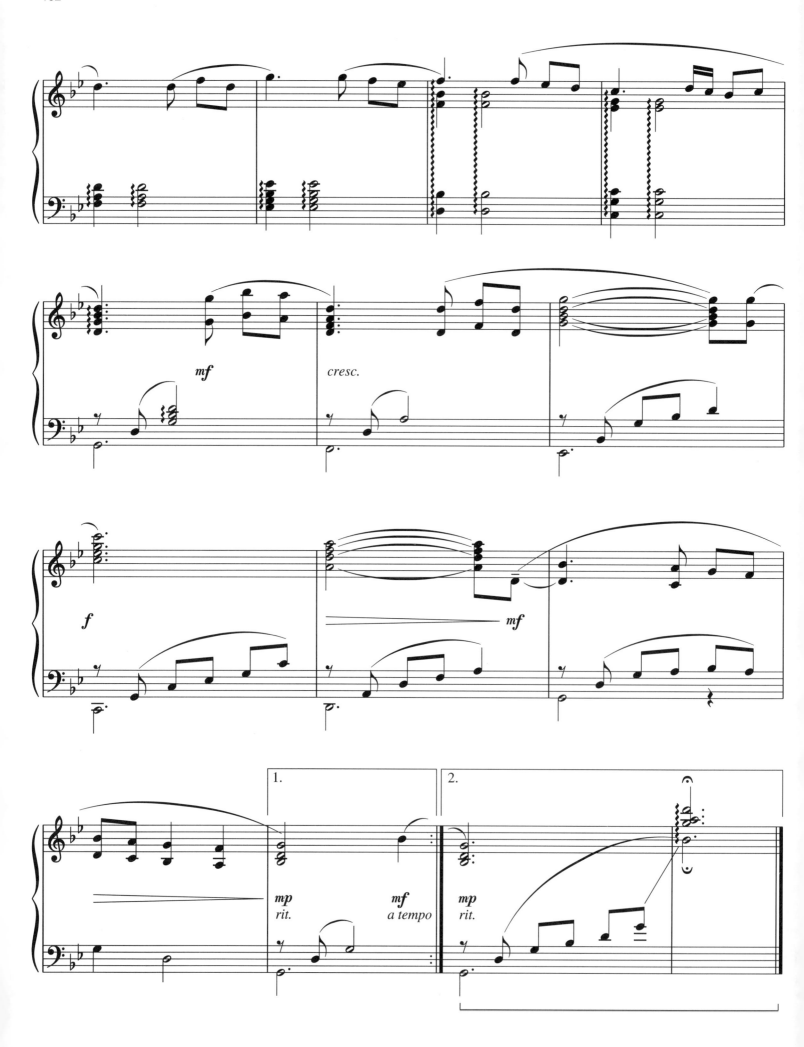

THE GODFATHER

(Love Theme)
from the Paramount Picture THE GODFATHER

By NINO ROTA

Slowly and expressively

BEAUTY AND THE BEAST

from Walt Disney's BEAUTY AND THE BEAST

Lyrics by HOWARD ASHMAN
Music by ALAN MENKEN

LOVE STORY
Theme from the Paramount Picture LOVE STORY

Music by FRANCIS LAI

Slowly

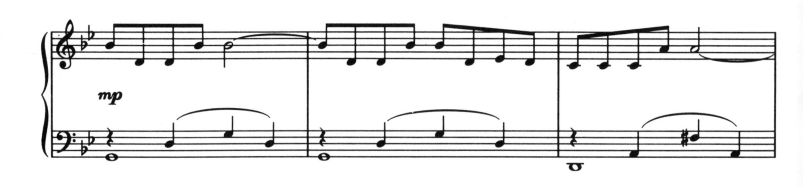

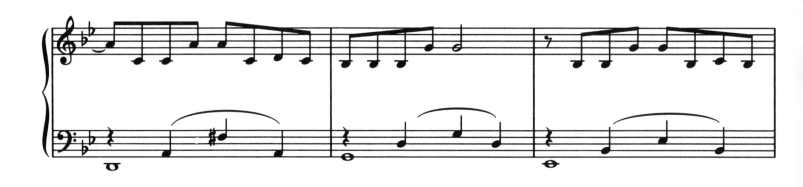

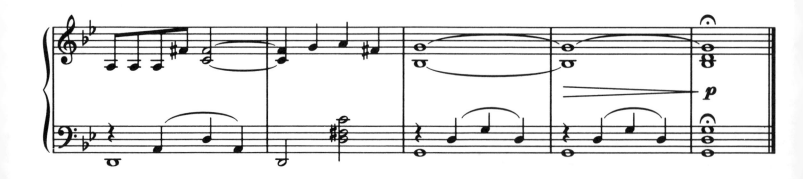

THE RAINBOW CONNECTION

from THE MUPPET MOVIE

Words and Music by PAUL WILLIAMS
and KENNETH L. ASCHER

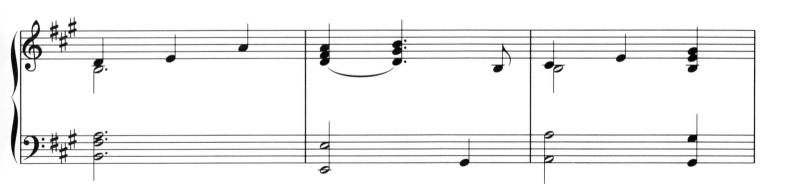

MY HEART WILL GO ON

(Love Theme from 'Titanic')

from the Paramount and Twentieth Century Fox Motion Picture TITANIC

Music by JAMES HORNER
Lyric by WILL JENNINGS

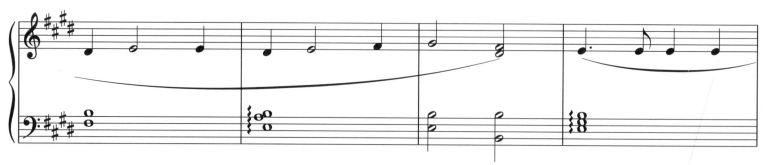

172

D.S. al Coda

CODA

THE WAY WE WERE
from the Motion Picture THE WAY WE WERE

Words by ALAN and MARILYN BERGMAN
Music by MARVIN HAMLISCH

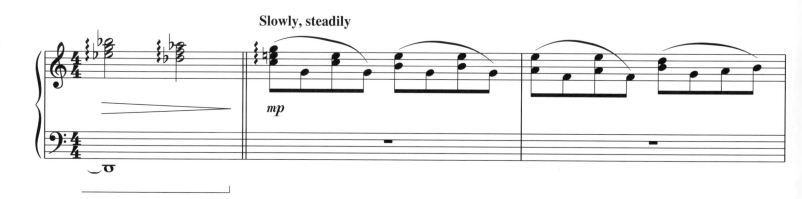

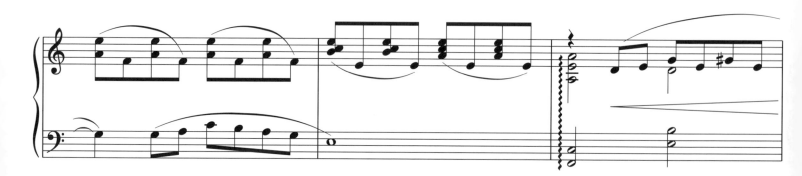

Boldly

BUTTERFLIES IN SPACE

By MICHAEL JONES

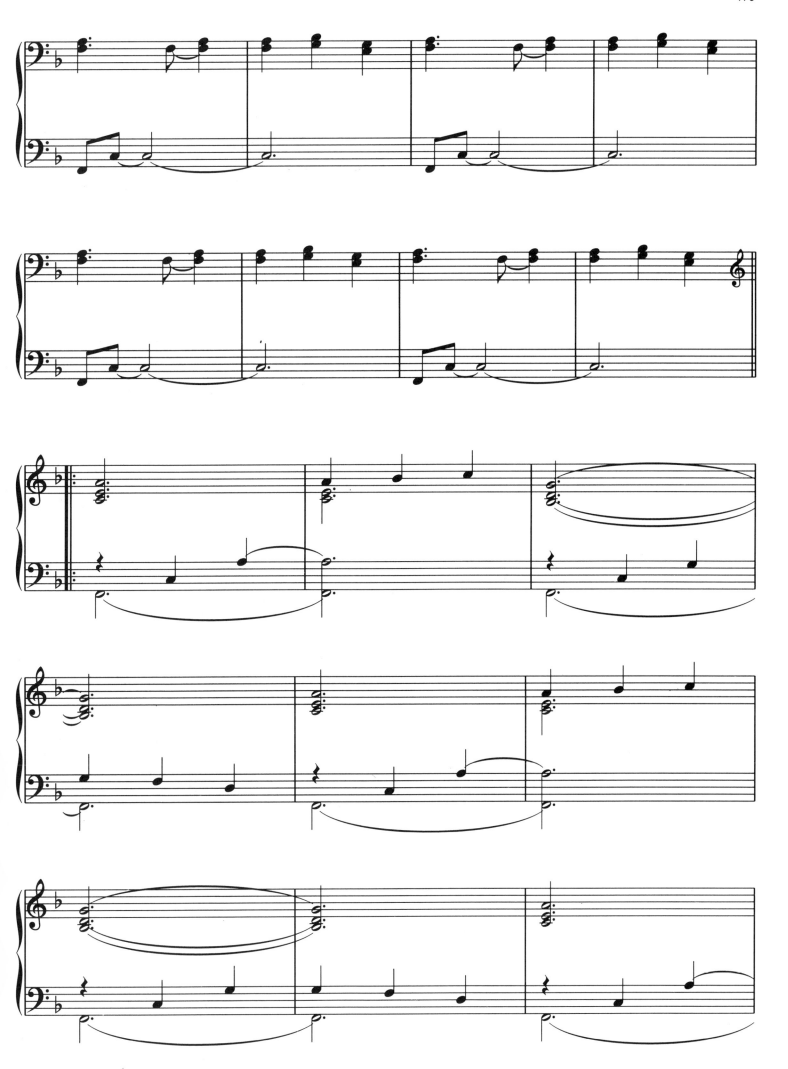

182

REVERIE

By DAVID LANZ

Original key of recording is E♭ minor.

8va

8va

8va bassa

8va

8va bassa

8va

8va bassa

PURPLE MOUNTAIN

By SCOTT COSSU

Tenderly

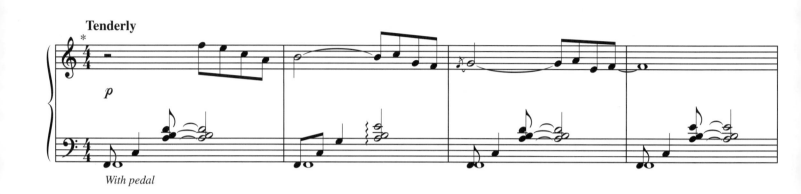

With pedal

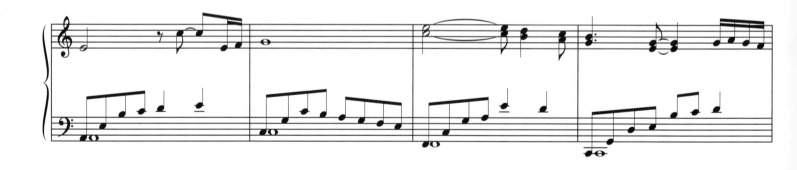

* Originally in the Key of D flat

To Coda

THE VELOCITY OF LOVE

By SUZANNE CIANI

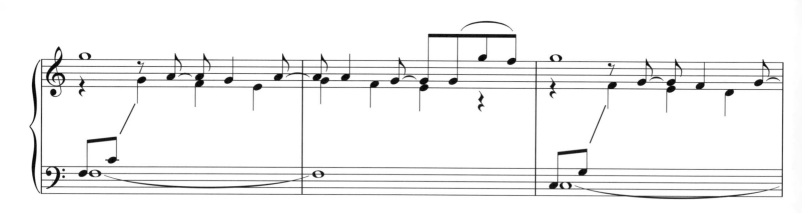

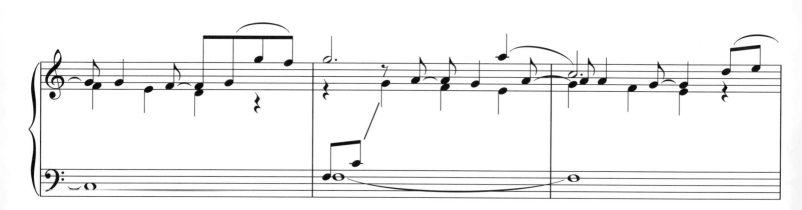

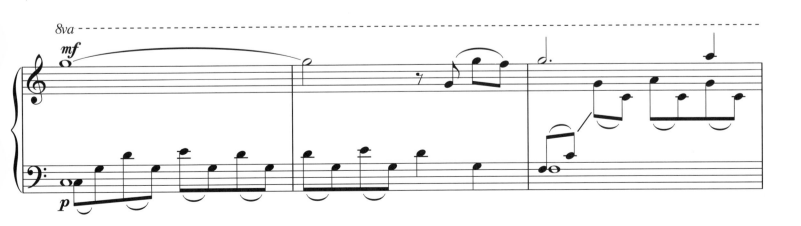

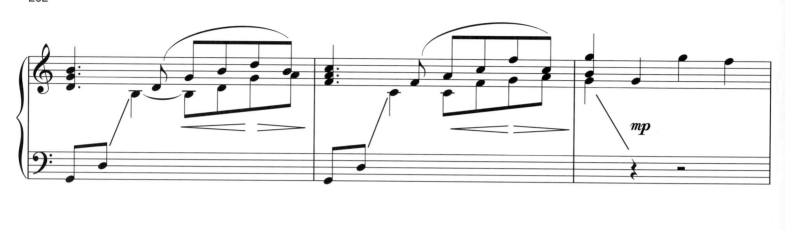

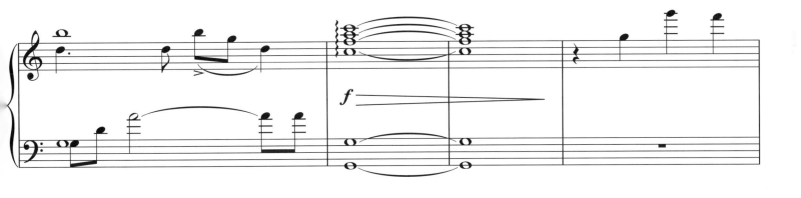

TOUCH OF PROMISE

By SPENCER BREWER

(Everything I Do)
I DO IT FOR YOU
from the Motion Picture ROBIN HOOD: PRINCE OF THIEVES

Words and Music by BRYAN ADAMS,
ROBERT JOHN LANGE and MICHAEL KAMEN

Slowly, with expression

With pedal

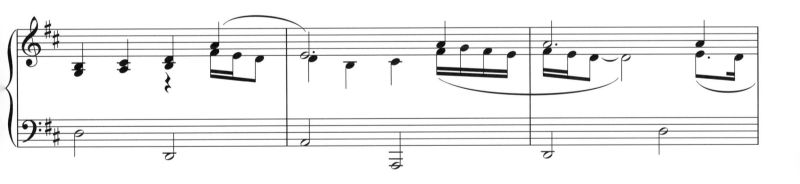

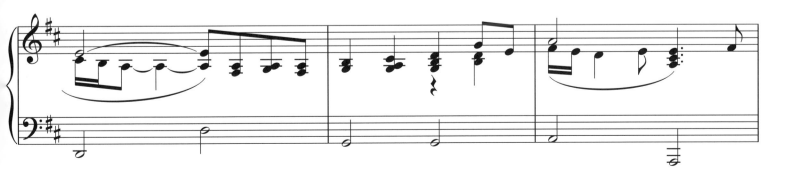

Slower, freely

Look into my eyes, you will see what you mean to me.
Search your heart, search your soul,
And when you find me there you'll search no more.
Don't tell me it's not worth fighting for.
You can't tell me, it's not worth dying for.
You know it's true, ev'rything I do, I do it for you.

Look into your heart, you will find there's nothing there to hide.
Take me as I am, take my life.
I would give it all I would sacrifice.
Don't tell me it's not worth fighting for.
I can't help it, there's nothing I want more.
You know it's true, ev'rything I do, I do it for you.

There's no love like your love, and no other could give more love.
There's no way, unless you're there all the time, all the way, yeah.

Oh you can't tell me it's not worth trying for.
I can't help it, there's nothing I want more.
Yeah, I would fight for you, I'd lie for you,
Walk the mile for you yeah, I'd die for you.
You know it's true, ev'rything I do, oh, oh, I do it for you.

ANGEL

Words and Music by
SARAH McLACHLAN

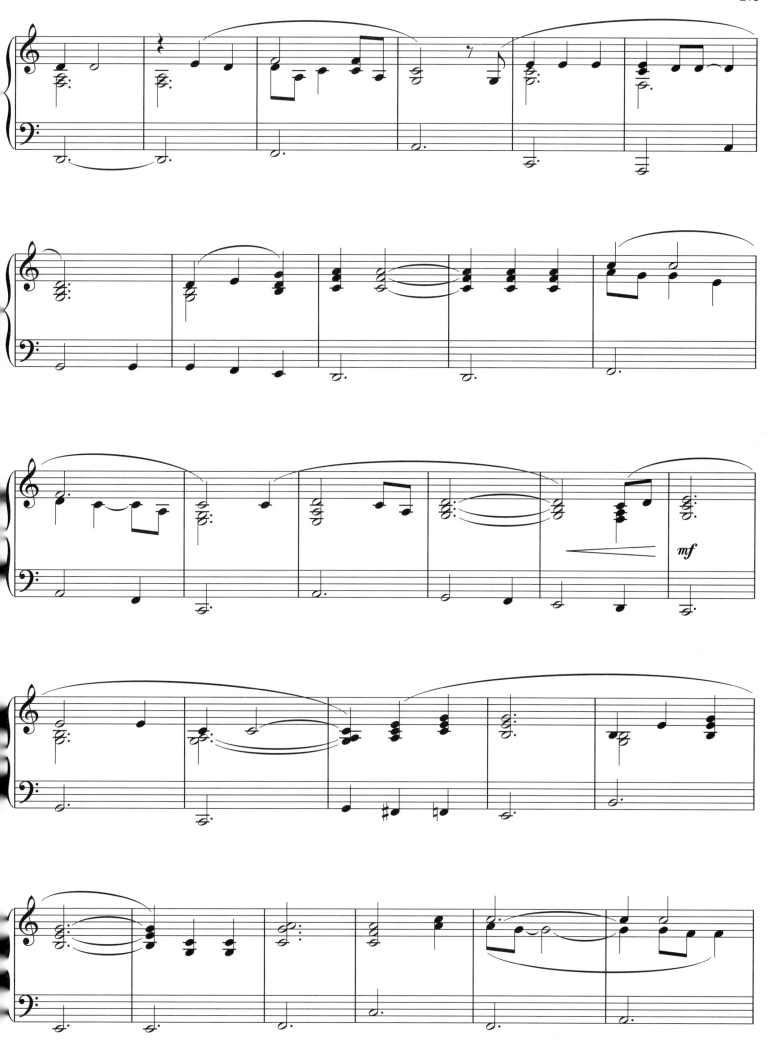

HERE, THERE AND EVERYWHERE

Words and Music by JOHN LENNON
and PAUL McCARTNEY

TEARS IN HEAVEN

Words and Music by ERIC CLAPTON
and WILL JENNINGS

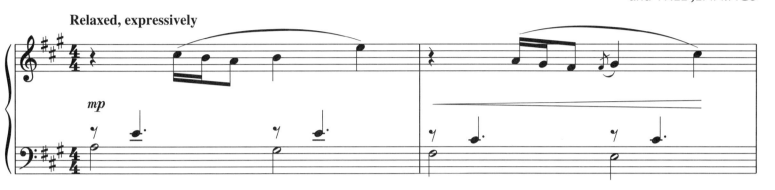

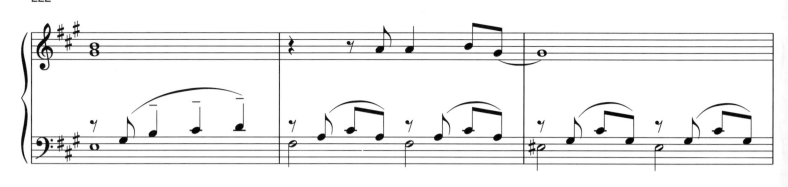

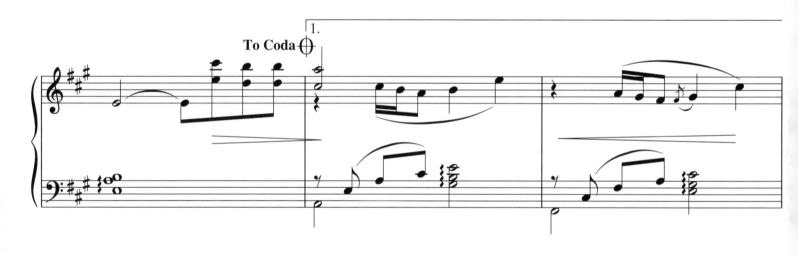

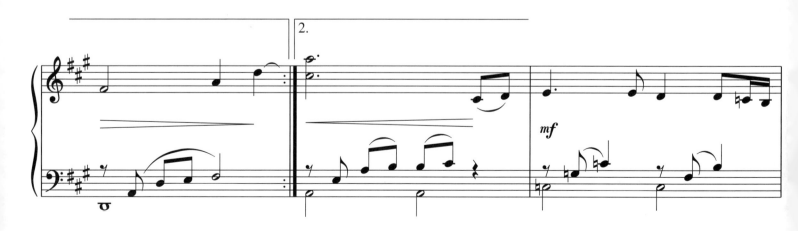

JUST THE WAY YOU ARE

Words and Music by
BILLY JOEL

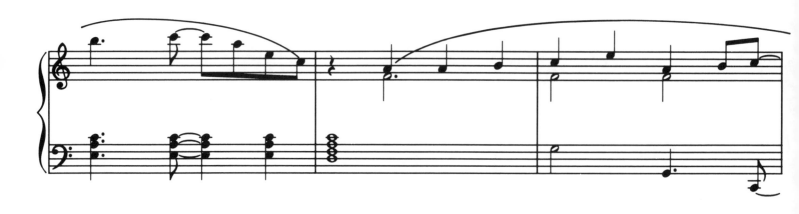

LONGER

Words and Music by
DAN FOGELBERG

Moderate ballad

AIN'T MISBEHAVIN'

Words by ANDY RAZAF
Music by THOMAS "FATS" WALLER
and HARRY BROOKS

IN A SENTIMENTAL MOOD

By DUKE ELLINGTON

MISTY

Music by ERROLL GARNER

Slowly and freely

Slow steady rhythm

Freely

245

MOON RIVER
from the Paramount Picture BREAKFAST AT TIFFANY'S

Words by JOHNNY MERCER
Music by HENRY MANCINI

Dreamy
Play freely throughout

MOONLIGHT IN VERMONT

Words and Music by JOHN BLACKBURN
and KARL SUESSDORF

With a steady beat

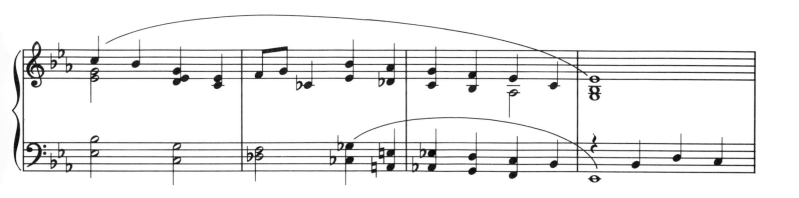

SOPHISTICATED LADY

from SOPHISTICATED LADIES

Words and Music by DUKE ELLINGTON,
IRVING MILLS and MITCHELL PARISH

WHEN I FALL IN LOVE

from ONE MINUTE TO ZERO

Words by EDWARD HEYMAN
Music by VICTOR YOUNG

With pedal

258

259

AULD LANG SYNE

Words by ROBERT BURNS
Traditional Scottish Melody

HAVAH NAGILAH

Traditional Hebrew

Fast Hora beat

THE STAR SPANGLED BANNER
(National Anthem)

Words by FRANCIS SCOTT KEY
Music by JOHN STAFFORD SMITH

With spirit

I LOVE YOU

from MEXICAN HAYRIDE

Words and Music by
COLE PORTER

Freely (Moderately)

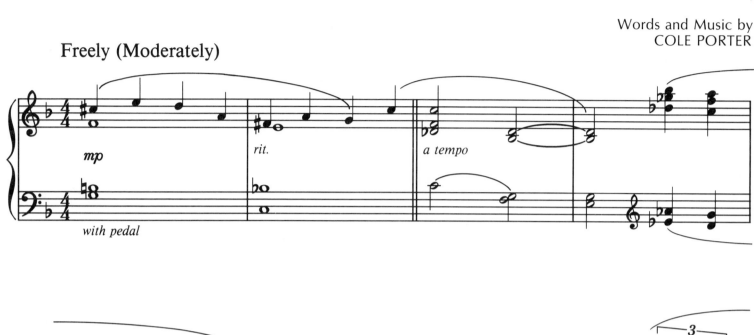

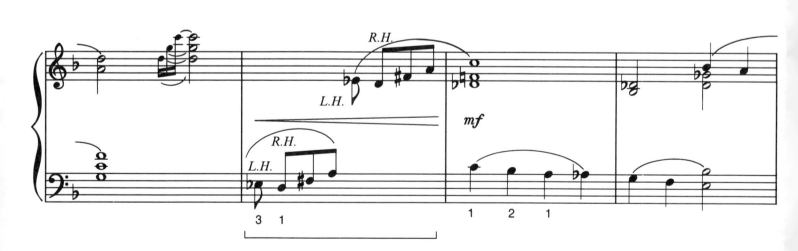

Steady rhythm (Moderately)

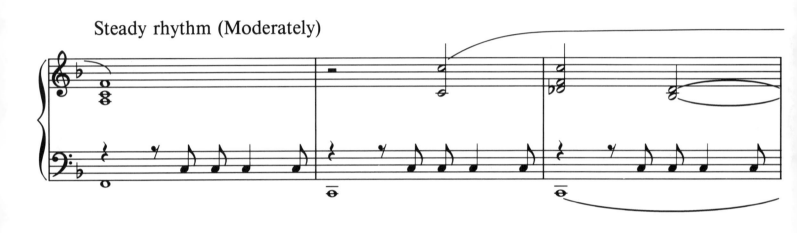

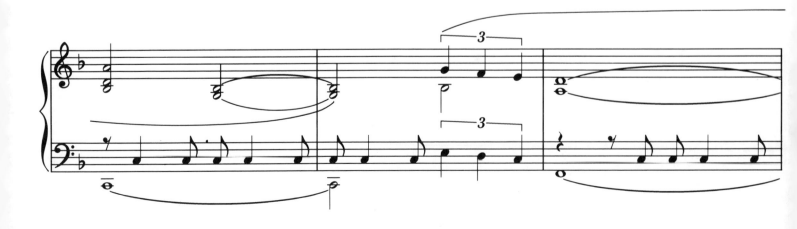

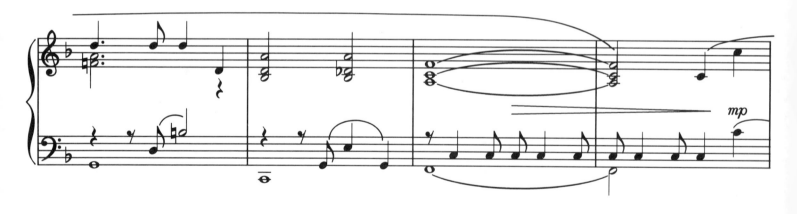

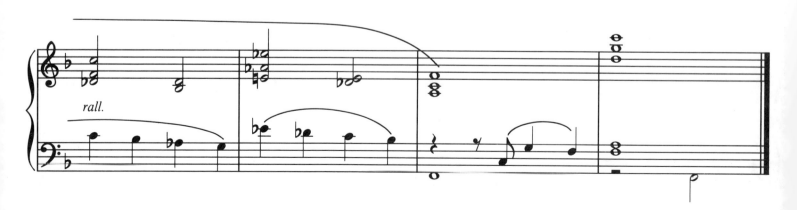